The
Plumdog
Path to Perfection

Also by Emma Chichester Clark

Plumdog

Plumdog titles for children

Love is My Favourite Thing!
Plenty of Love to Go Round

The
Plumdog
Path to Perfection

Emma Chichester Clark

JONATHAN CAPE
LONDON

Published by Jonathan Cape 2016

2 4 6 8 10 9 7 5 3 1

Copyright illustrations © Emma Chichester Clark 2016

Emma Chichester Clark has asserted her right under the Copyright, Designs
and Patents Act 1988 to be identified as the author of this work

The author acknowledges the kind permission of Liberty Ltd to utilise the endpaper artwork

First published in Great Britain in 2016 by Jonathan Cape

www.vintage-books.co.uk

Jonathan Cape is part of the Penguin Random House group of companies
whose addresses can be found at global.penguinrandomhouse.com

A CIP catalogue record for this book is available from the British Library

ISBN 9781910702215

Printed and bound in China by C&C Offset Printing Co., Ltd

Perfect

Character

Simplicity of character
is the most natural
result of profound thought.

Hazlitt

No great mind
has ever existed
without a touch
of madness.

Aristotle

Everyone enjoys the company
of a soul who is light.

Unknown

Mix a little foolishness
with your prudence.
It's good to look silly
at the right moment.

Horace

The two most important places to keep tidy are my mind and my heart.

Unknown

To be old and wise you must first
be young and stupid.

Unknown

How glorious it is
and how painful
to be an exception.

Alfred de Musset

Almost all absurdity of character
arises from the imitation
of those we cannot resemble.

Samuel Johnson

It is good to do things for others, especially if no one knows about it.

Unknown

In trying to get our own way
we should remember that kisses
are sweeter than whine.

Unknown

He is extremely clever who learns a trick from
someone else's mistake.

Anonymous

A smile at the right moment
is as welcome as a
glass of water in the desert.

Anon

Always act as though you are
wearing an invisible crown.

Unknown

Perfect
Friendship

Talking to your best friend is sometimes
all the therapy you need.

Unknown

A friend is someone who knows
the song in your heart and
will sing it back to you when
you've forgotten the words.

Camus

There are no such things as strangers,
only friends we haven't yet met.

Unknown

Real friends don't care if you're a little different.

Unknown

Hospitality is making your guests
feel at home even if you
wish they were.

Unknown

Guests always give pleasure, if not the arrival, the departure.

Unknown

The key is to keep company
with people who uplift you,
whose presence calls forth
your best.

Epictetus

Certain flaws are necessary for the whole.
It would seem strange if old friends
lacked certain quirks.

Goethe

Some of the people in our lives are gifts.
Others are simply lessons.

Unknown

Wishing to be friends is quick work
but friendship is a slow ripening fruit.

Aristotle

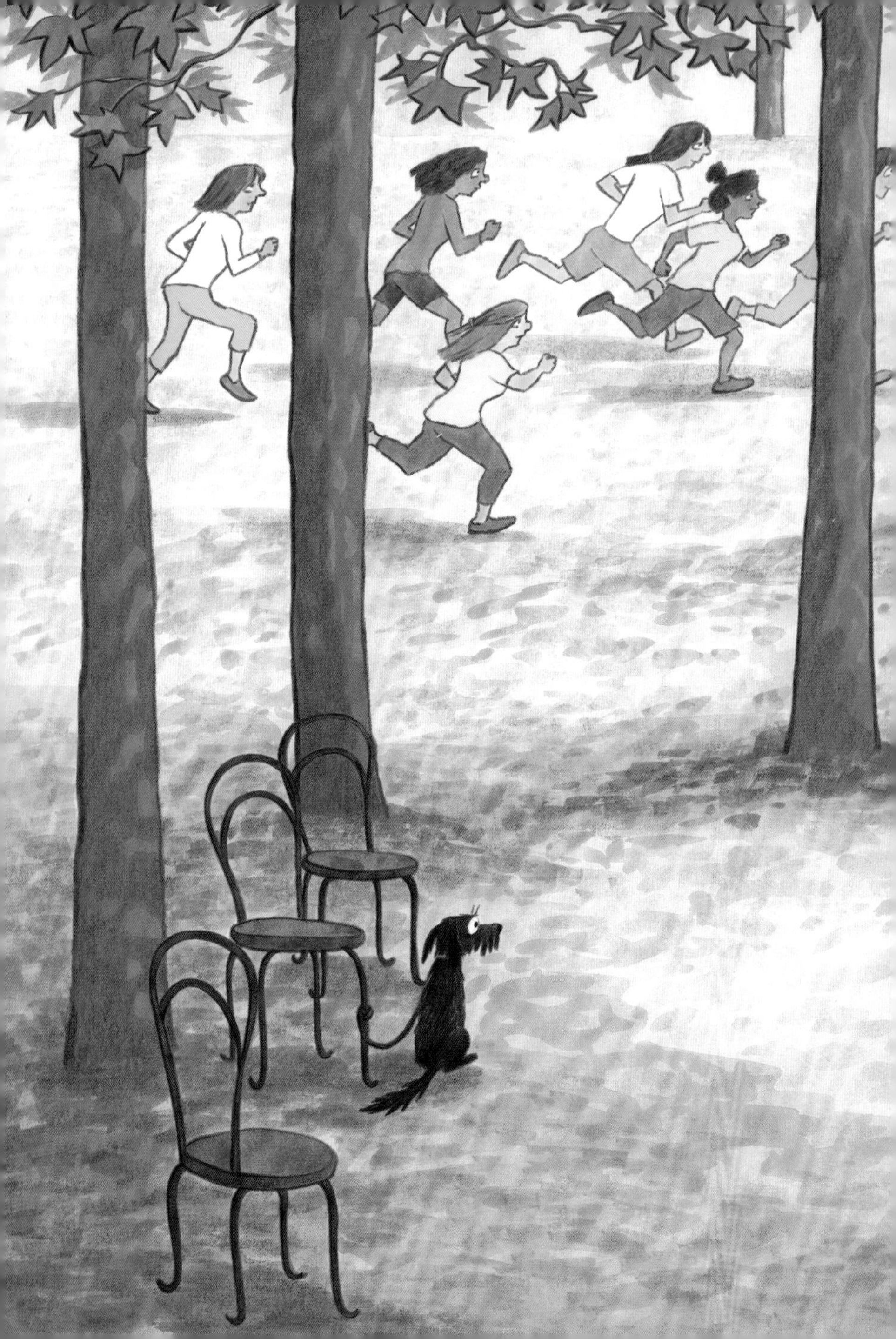

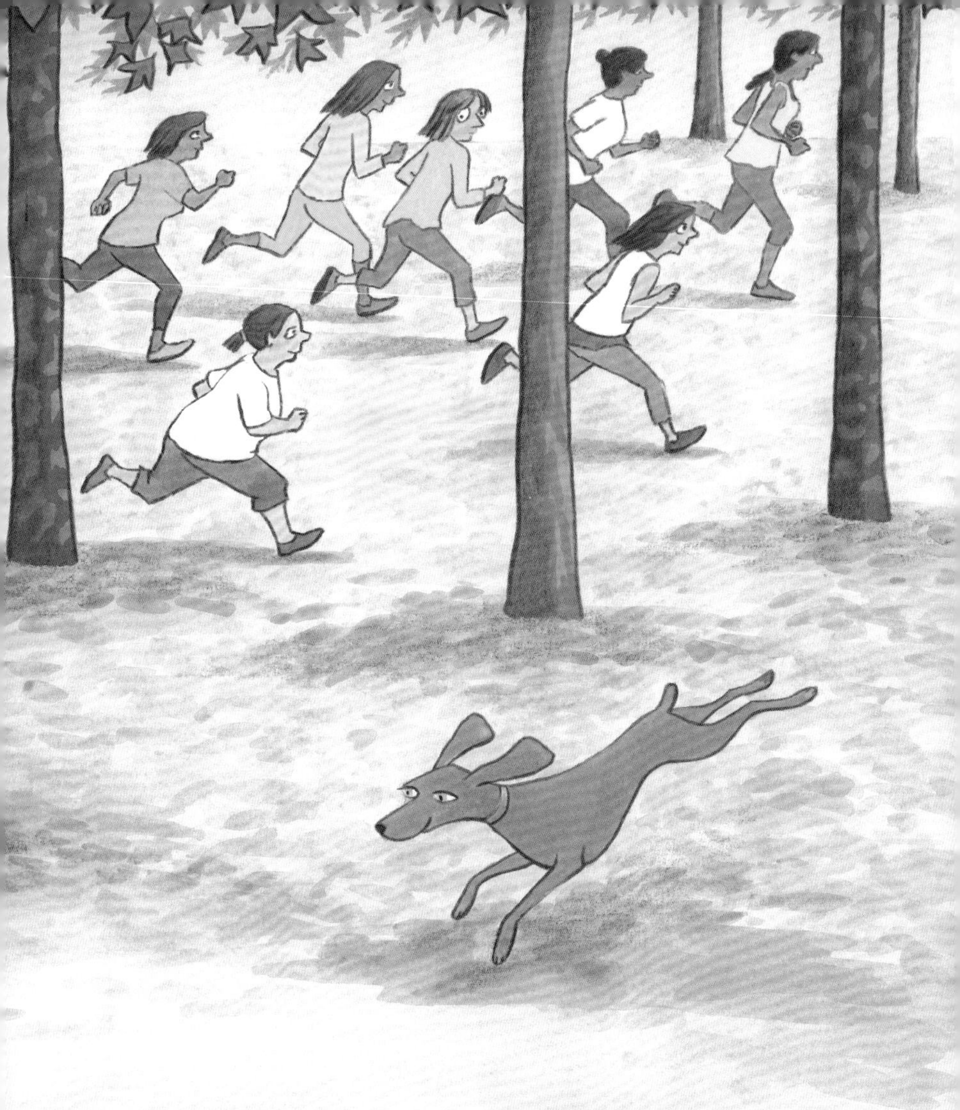

A real friend is one who runs towards you
when the rest of the world runs away.

Unknown

Friends are God's way of taking care of us.

Unknown

Perfect
Love

Love reckons hours for months,
days for years and every little
absence is an age.

John Dryden

Do not feel you should subdue your passions.
Sometimes it's too difficult.

Unknown

Do everything with love.

Corinthians

When the thing that makes you happy is someone else's happiness, that's love.

Anonymous

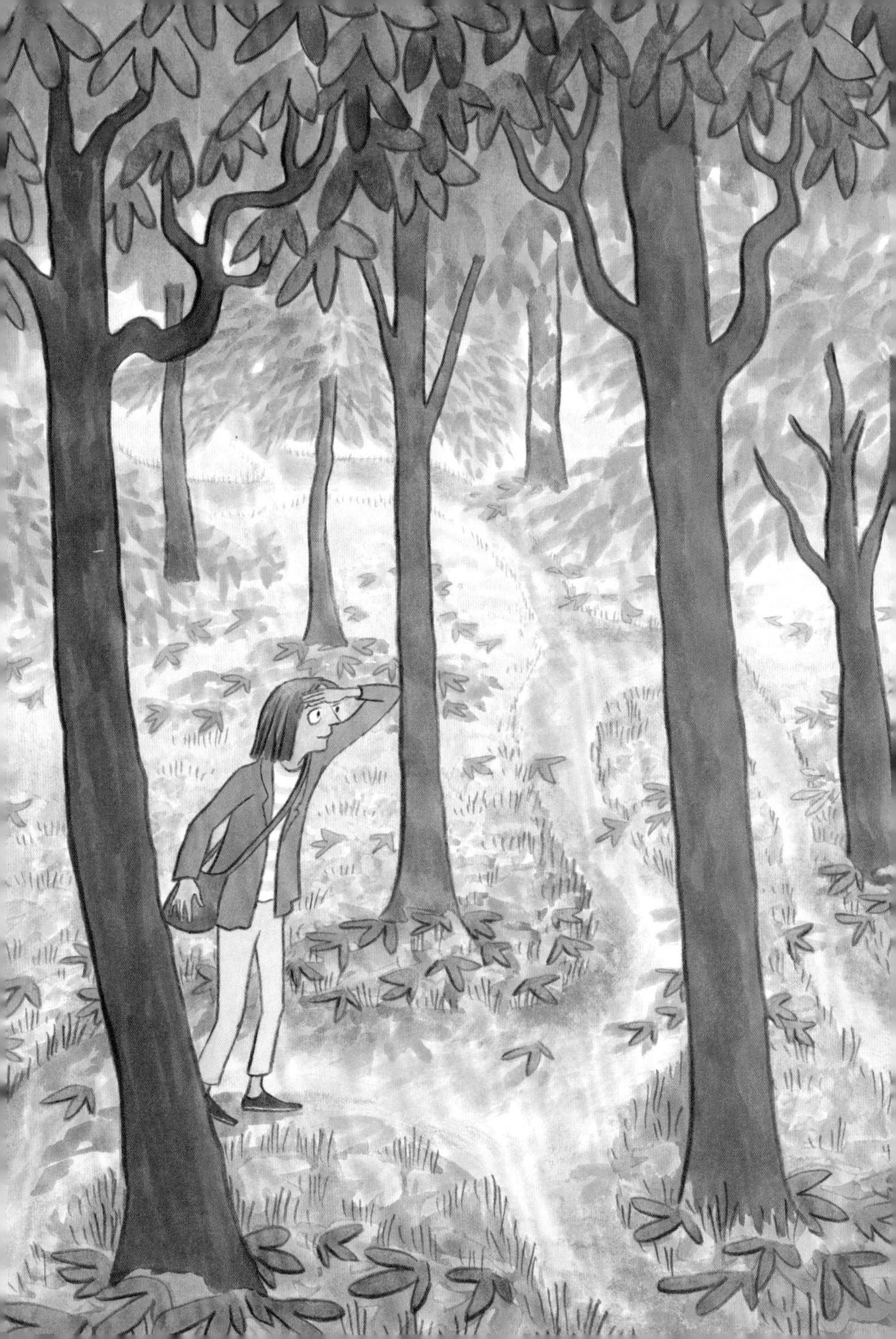

People who are meant to be
together find their way back—
they may make a few detours
but they're never lost.

Unknown

You may look in the mirror and see flaws but
someone else looks at you and sees someone they love.

Unknown

Let us be grateful to people who make us happy. They are the charming gardeners who make our souls blossom.

Marcel Proust

Real love comes less through words and more
through pure feeling.

Unknown

Not Absolutely

Perfect

The keenest sorrow

is to recognise ourselves

as the sole cause

of all our adversities.

Sophocles

Don't let a hard lesson harden your heart.
Anonymous

Problems come when we act without thinking or sometimes when we think without acting.

Unknown

Anyone who has never
made a mistake has never
tried anything new.

Einstein

Learn to trust the journey even when
you don't know where it is going.

Unknown

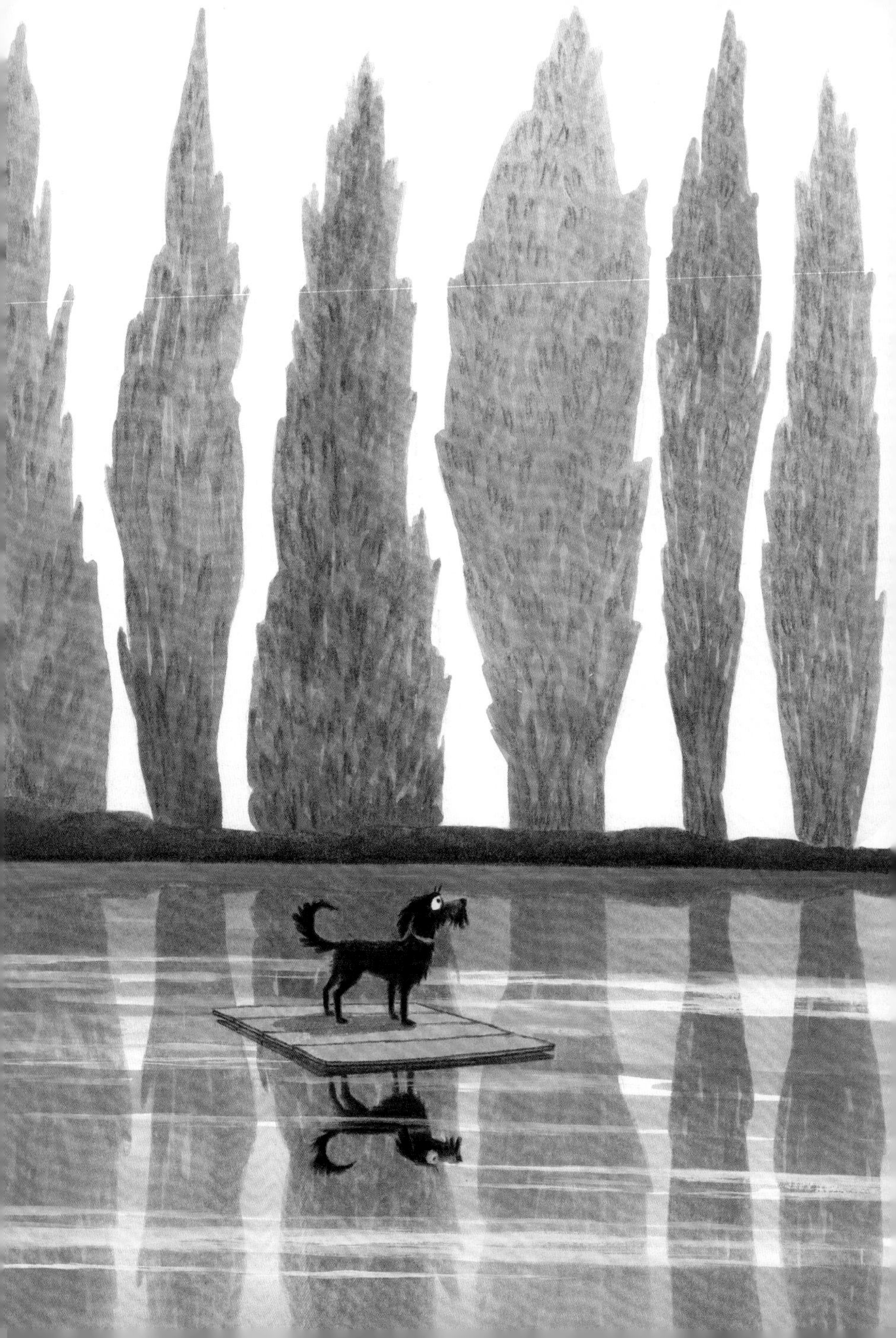

There are more things
to alarm us than to harm
us, and we suffer more often
in apprehension than reality.

Seneca.

To him who is in fear —
everything rustles.

Sophocles

Much speech is one thing.
Well-timed speech is another.

Sophocles

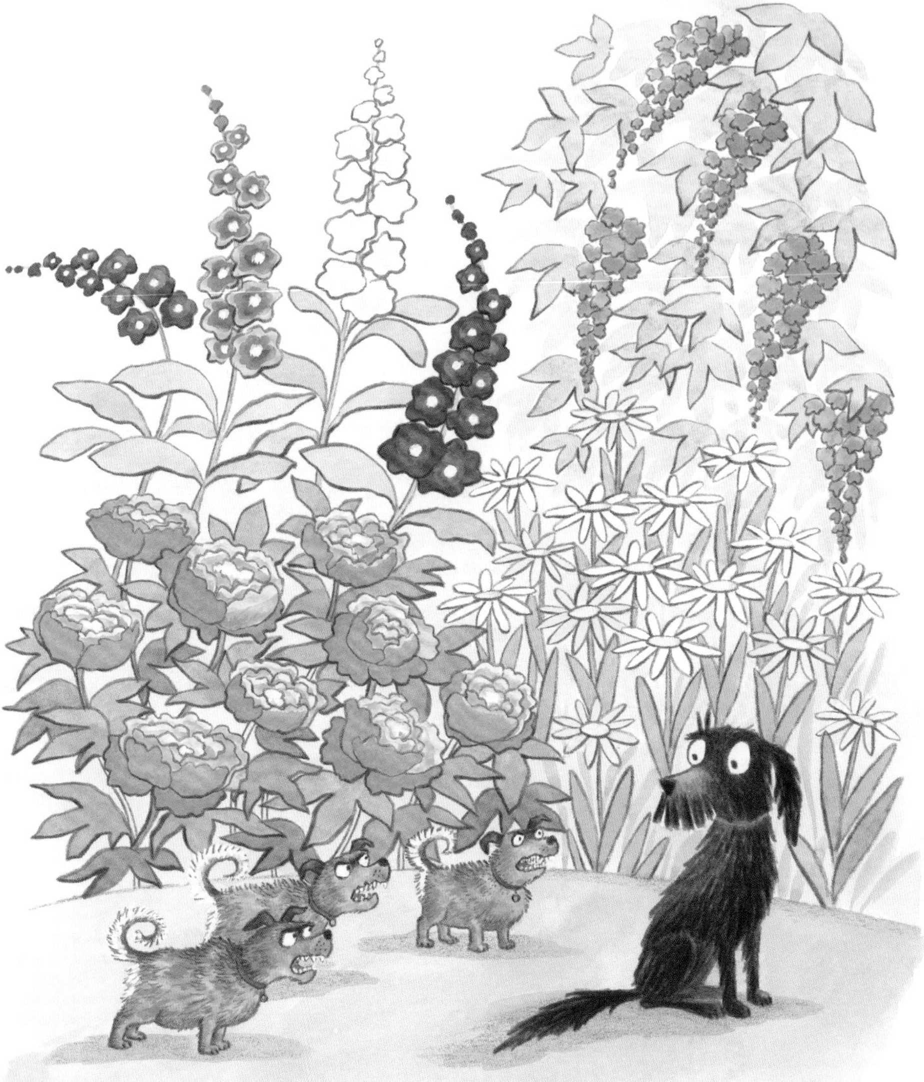

You don't have to understand everything. Everything doesn't understand you.

Just accept it and move on.

Unknown

It may be that your whole purpose in life is to serve
as a warning to others.

Anon

Perfect Life

Giving is a lifestyle.

Unknown

You can change your view of life
simply by choosing
to sit in a different chair.

Unknown

The moon and the stars belong to everyone,
even me.

Unknown

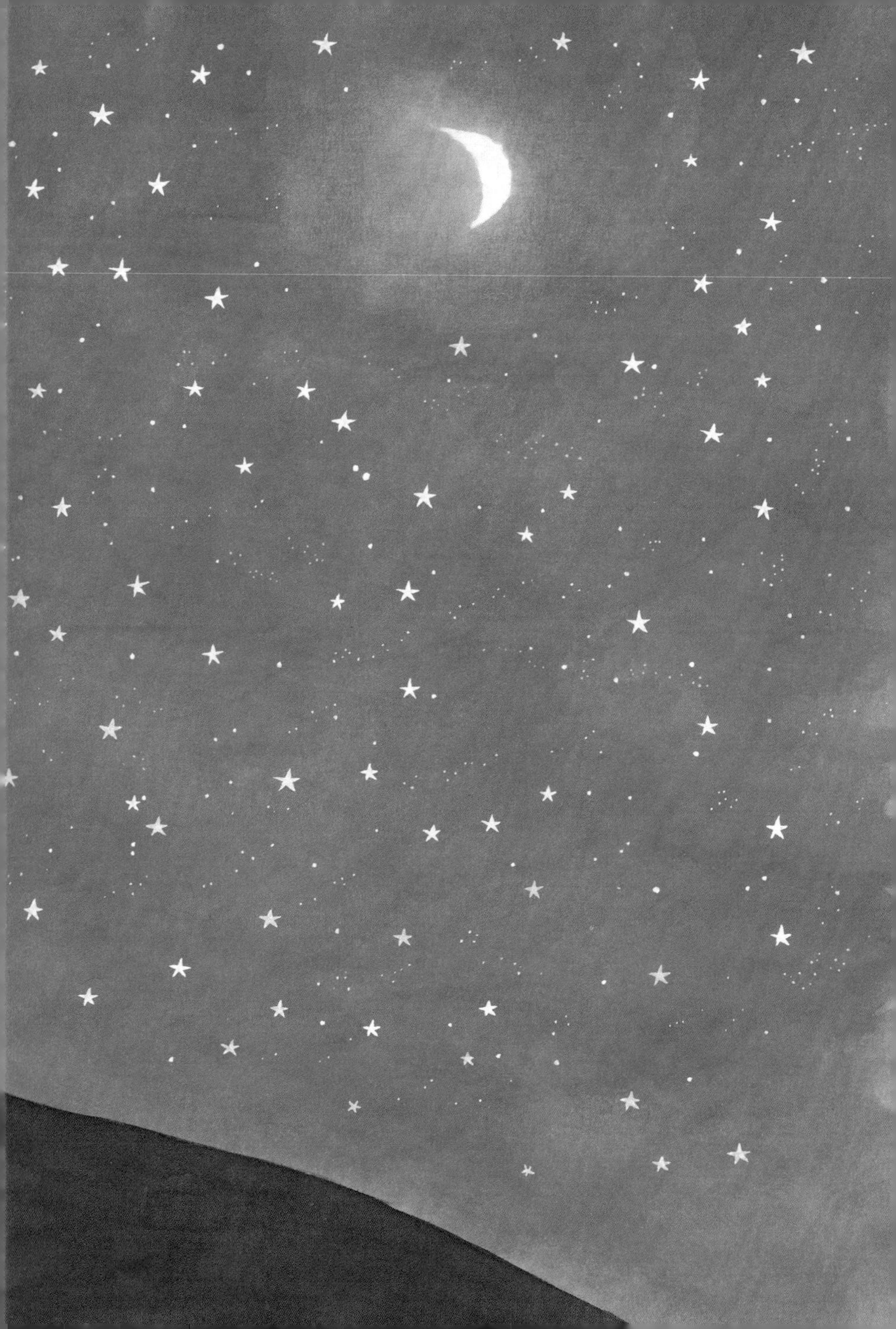

Try to be present
and listen to the person
who is talking to you instead
of wondering what is going
to happen next.

Unknown

You can wait forever for the storm to pass
or you can rush out and lark about in the rain.

Unknown

Music is part of us and either ennobles or
degrades our behaviour.

Boethius

Just living is not enough.
One must have sunshine,
freedom, and a little flower.

Hans Christian Andersen

Wherever you go, go with all your heart.

Confucius

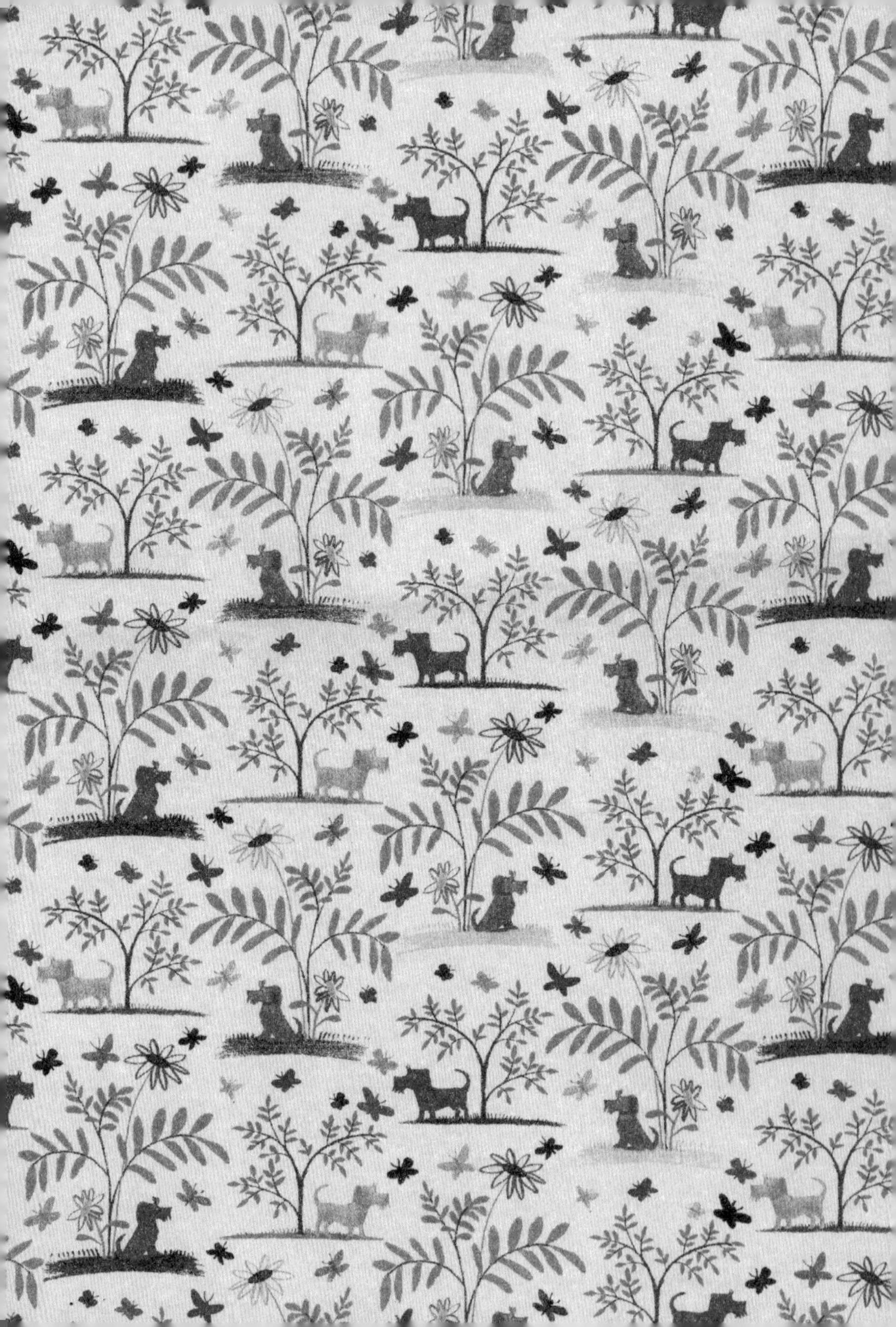